Download Festival Puzzle Book

Celebrating 20 years of Rock.

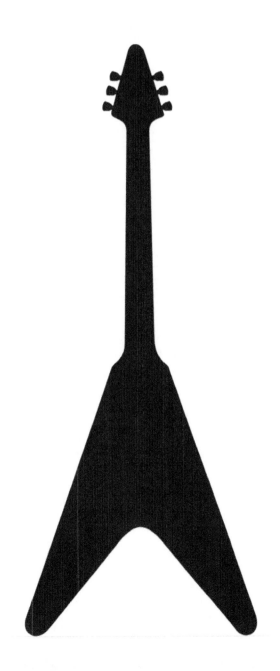

First paperback edition December 2022

Front cover Image by Pete Linforth from Pixabay

www.GamblingAddictionExplained.com

Download Festival

Celebrating 20 years of Rock.

Download Festival is a British-created Rock and Heavy Metal festival held annually at the Donington Park motorsport circuit in Leicestershire, England since 2003.

Download Festival is the biggest and most loved U.K rock and heavy metal festival and was conceived as a follow up to the Monsters of Rock festivals which had been held previously at the Donington Park circuit between 1980 and 1996.

It appears the name Download was chosen for the festival for two reasons. The concept of downloading music was a hot topic at the time, and generally seen as seedy or, at best, unethical. Rock and heavy metal music has always been seen as a rebelious genre of music. The 2003 festival tickets had a code on them, which would allow festival goers to download tracks from the bands which had played that weekend.

The original Download festival in 2003 was a two day event growning over the years and to celebrate its 20th anniversay in 2023 the event is held over five days.

The following pages consist of a crossword puzzle for each Download year based upon bands playing that year. Following the crossword puzzle for that year is a word search with the same band names hidden within. You cannot get the band names without solving the crossword. (Unless you cheat and look at the answers at the back of the book).

Even the most hardened rockers need some time to kick back and chill, what better way than some fun, Download themed puzzles.

Enjoy.

Download Festival 2003

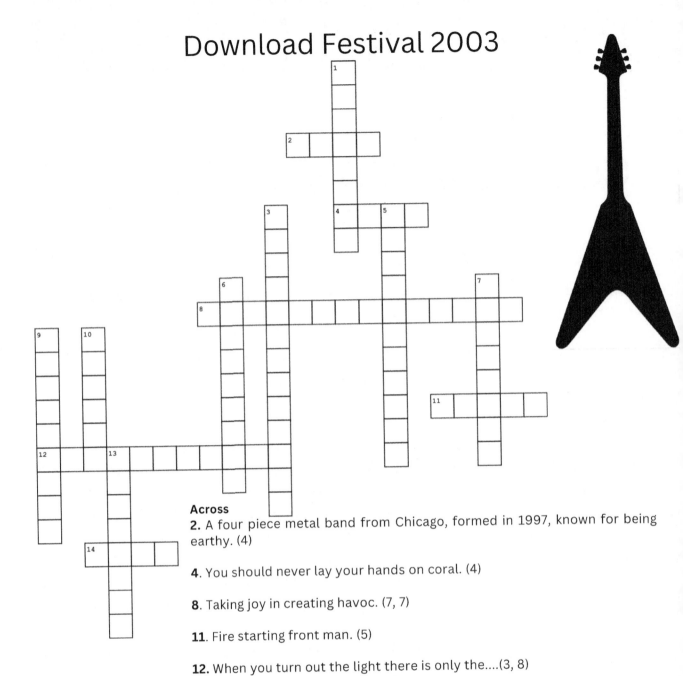

Across

2. A four piece metal band from Chicago, formed in 1997, known for being earthy. (4)

4. You should never lay your hands on coral. (4)

8. Taking joy in creating havoc. (7, 7)

11. Fire starting front man. (5)

12. When you turn out the light there is only the....(3, 8)

14. It has zero effects. (4)

Down

1. Monty Python had one of these for Silly Walks. (8)

3. What do you get when you combine an infamous criminal with a blonde bombshell from the 50's and early 60's. (7, 6)

5. A vanishing act. (11)

6. Despite being disordered it was agreed that he was the "Best Druid". (9)

7. A fire breathing she monster in Greek mythology having the head of a lion, a goats body, and a serpent's tail from Ohio.(8)

9. Portuguese word for grave. (9)

10. Once, once more, and once again. (6)

13. Who would have thought a Tone Deaf band could be this good? (8)

Download Festival 2003

See if you can find the acts from Download 2003 in the word search below. It is tricky though, words can e in any direction in a straight line, front or backward.

Z	C	D	D	Y	M	E	N	E	H	C	R	A	E	G	Z
B	S	M	A	R	I	L	Y	N	M	A	N	S	O	N	I
T	H	L	A	B	E	J	G	I	W	O	U	D	R	T	Z
S	S	I	O	I	S	C	Y	S	F	Z	I	E	H	V	T
W	Y	O	S	O	R	R	N	X	F	S	E	G	K	H	A
D	Y	S	L	H	T	O	A	E	T	F	I	A	E	F	A
T	E	J	A	S	A	R	N	U	C	L	G	D	R	U	K
P	D	F	I	R	I	D	R	M	E	S	A	F	D	G	V
U	F	N	T	A	U	B	O	D	A	R	E	I	V	A	A
S	I	K	M	O	E	T	T	W	K	I	O	N	N	C	I
M	F	I	L	D	N	N	L	N	S	S	D	E	A	U	F
L	H	L	E	S	E	E	E	U	L	F	C	E	F	V	D
C	H	H	I	L	C	S	S	A	P	I	A	Q	N	Q	E
D	W	C	O	N	S	Q	V	V	R	E	J	L	N	L	D
U	Z	I	A	Q	T	E	D	H	S	Q	S	V	L	N	A
B	V	R	E	S	R	E	T	P	O	C	I	L	E	H	M

Download Festival 2004

Across

5. Nu metal band from Bakersfield, California, who are here to stay (4)

7. Cyclone celebrations. (9,5)

9. Without these, Whiskey could not be made. (3,10)

13. Alice drinks Malt Whiskey in the jar. (9)

14. You need to follow this to get it right (11)

15. City of the Moon. (5)

16. Every electric guitar needs one (9)

Down

1. Clifford Lathe had a mucky crib. (6,2,5)

2. Not to be confused with Curly, Larry, and Moe. (3,7)

3. The clown. (9)

4. The layers are all mixed up. (6)

6. Citizens of the U S of A who need a wash. (5, 9)

8. The first stitch in knitting. (8)

10. They had an album without any colour in 2007. (3,5)

11. Presidents of the United States of America love these from a can. (7)

12. The older I get the longer it takes to. (7)

Download Festival 2004

See if you can find the acts from Download 2004 in the word search below. It is tricky though, words can be in any direction in a straight line, front or backward.

L	C	R	A	D	L	E	O	F	F	I	L	T	H	N	G	L	W	V
M	E	C	J	Y	T	R	A	P	E	N	A	C	I	R	R	U	H	I
D	A	E	T	H	E	D	I	S	T	I	L	L	E	R	S	C	P	B
Y	Y	C	S	Y	A	S	C	X	R	E	I	F	I	L	P	M	A	A
U	Z	J	H	K	Z	V	E	U	J	S	L	H	A	Z	C	W	V	F
O	D	X	R	I	L	M	O	V	W	B	L	U	H	Y	X	D	G	Z
E	J	D	U	N	N	Q	X	X	I	G	L	I	D	B	Z	S	O	P
O	C	P	A	L	S	E	P	I	W	H	D	M	P	X	K	E	I	E
K	Q	I	O	P	E	T	H	S	R	I	E	N	E	K	X	G	V	A
W	W	L	D	K	L	I	L	E	N	T	O	H	F	X	N	O	K	C
L	J	Z	N	N	V	A	C	G	A	I	E	N	T	V	H	O	C	H
X	P	R	W	K	Y	O	P	L	T	D	S	W	N	O	I	T	T	E
G	O	Q	G	E	V	L	L	C	K	O	I	C	O	K	U	S	Z	S
K	W	W	R	E	A	I	U	K	F	F	W	X	H	N	U	E	F	J
R	D	O	R	C	C	R	M	K	T	F	Y	D	Y	U	O	H	L	O
M	E	A	E	A	T	B	D	Z	H	P	N	V	E	D	Z	T	S	I
U	R	G	F	S	D	Z	K	R	A	P	N	I	K	N	I	L	J	F
D	S	S	N	Z	S	N	A	C	I	R	E	M	A	Y	T	R	I	D
Z	B	I	D	X	C	T	F	K	R	P	P	Z	I	E	H	T	B	D

Download Festival 2005

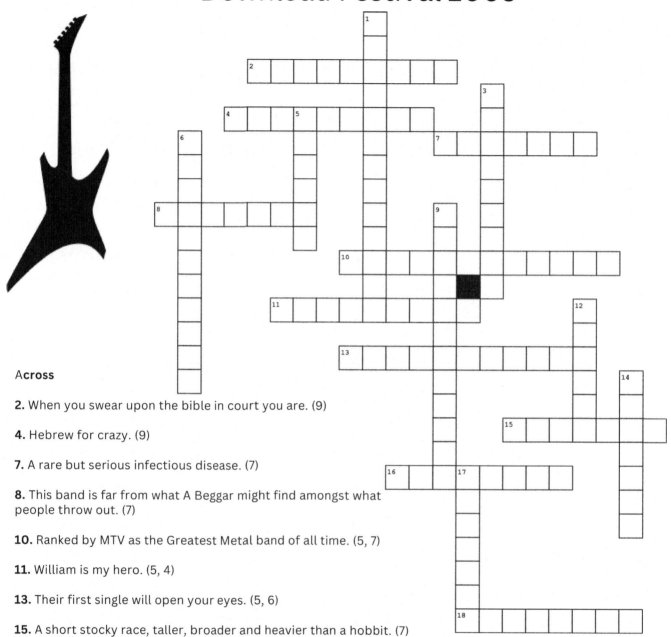

Across

2. When you swear upon the bible in court you are. (9)

4. Hebrew for crazy. (9)

7. A rare but serious infectious disease. (7)

8. This band is far from what A Beggar might find amongst what people throw out. (7)

10. Ranked by MTV as the Greatest Metal band of all time. (5, 7)

11. William is my hero. (5, 4)

13. Their first single will open your eyes. (5, 6)

15. A short stocky race, taller, broader and heavier than a hobbit. (7)

16. A large extinct elephant like mammal. (8)

18. This bands long standing mascot embodies see no evil, hear no evil, speak no evil. (8)

Down

1. Whipping Mary. (8, 5)

3. Lemmy's band. (9)

5. You should always wear one of these on your head when riding. (6)

6. When all said and done these are considered by many as the pioneers of grindcore. (6, 5)

9. Mythical beasts flying around the capital of Japan. (5, 7)

12. Awarding winning welsh rock band who sang about Buck Rogers, (6)

14. Dig it up. (7)

17. Latin word for where three roads met. (7)

Download Festival 2005

ee if you can find the acts from Download 2005 in the word search below. It is tricky though, words can be in any direction in a straight line, front or backward.

R	T	E	P	E	I	Y	L	T	U	T	C	V	M	D	A	M	W	K
P	S	T	X	L	N	O	D	O	T	S	A	M	Y	Z	L	E	Y	F
O	E	T	X	F	E	E	D	E	R	W	F	B	A	H	T	G	F	V
D	G	R	F	C	Y	J	I	R	G	L	I	F	T	T	E	A	E	J
W	A	I	L	Z	H	I	H	K	K	L	V	A	U	A	R	D	H	Y
A	B	V	O	K	Y	T	B	T	L	E	E	K	X	N	B	E	I	B
S	R	I	G	G	M	O	A	Y	A	D	T	K	K	T	R	T	M	M
O	A	U	G	P	J	N	I	B	M	O	U	R	H	H	I	H	O	M
F	G	M	I	H	B	D	N	L	B	M	R	A	P	R	D	P	T	V
C	H	T	N	L	O	L	A	S	H	A	G	E	Y	A	G	O	O	U
W	L	J	G	L	G	P	M	U	Q	G	S	J	D	X	E	M	R	M
U	F	Q	M	L	A	O	C	L	U	H	C	K	Y	N	E	W	H	D
L	J	P	O	N	S	R	Q	H	H	Z	E	H	C	D	U	G	E	N
P	E	L	L	U	J	L	S	E	U	I	O	L	O	A	U	Q	A	G
G	K	E	L	K	T	E	X	C	Q	G	E	Y	M	B	L	C	D	Z
Y	I	N	Y	P	M	W	D	U	B	M	R	P	C	E	U	B	N	S
O	G	O	Y	Y	C	X	L	E	D	N	H	K	P	V	T	R	K	V
O	H	S	N	O	G	A	R	D	O	Y	K	O	T	G	E	N	Q	V
W	D	W	A	R	V	E	S	H	T	R	A	E	N	U	Y	H	E	P

Download Festival 2006

Across

1. You must be Joking Kelli. (7, 4)

3. Crazy (5)

9. More bandages need applying. (8, 7)

13. You do not want one stuck in your throat. (8)

14. You need the right one for the right job. (4)

15. The side opposite that toward which a person is looking. (9)

16. One of Downloads favourite reggae metal bands from Newport, Wales. (8)

Down

2. I used to love her singing Nurses Song. (4, 1, 5)

4. A very large building of worship, usually built from stone. (9)

5. To grip or clench something. (6)

6. You need to pass this if you want to play in the band. (3, 8)

7. From beginning to end. (4, 5, 2, 4)

8. With everybody in the place they were soon out of space. (3, 7)

10. ....is always before dawn. (7, 4)

11. Seattle band who's debut album was called Facelift. (5, 2, 6)

12. In walks Shirkari. (5, 8)

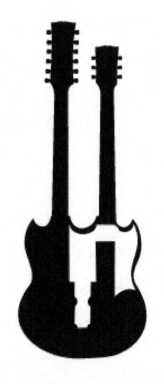

Download Festival 2006

See if you can find the acts from Download 2006 in the word search below. It is tricky though, words can be in any direction in a straight line, front or backward.

R	M	X	L	T	S	A	L	O	T	T	S	R	I	F	M	O	R	F
L	W	A	F	M	R	U	O	H	T	S	E	K	R	A	D	S	Y	V
A	L	J	D	L	Y	Z	M	J	T	E	N	O	B	H	S	I	F	Z
L	Z	L	K	N	O	I	T	I	D	U	A	E	H	T	F	V	O	P
I	O	V	K	P	T	L	I	F	P	Q	D	Y	W	Q	Z	E	E	F
C	L	H	A	F	K	I	R	A	K	I	H	S	R	E	T	N	E	C
E	G	B	O	K	M	T	Y	G	C	I	N	A	M	K	V	G	E	X
I	B	L	E	E	D	I	N	G	T	H	R	O	U	G	H	K	S	D
N	X	L	N	V	T	H	E	S	V	E	X	B	X	I	O	E	E	R
C	F	Q	L	A	R	D	E	H	T	A	C	S	L	J	S	D	U	Y
H	C	L	U	T	C	H	G	S	M	A	A	S	G	O	I	O	R	G
A	O	P	N	M	L	I	H	N	F	T	G	N	R	S	W	W	F	I
I	X	L	B	U	D	F	Y	N	C	U	I	N	D	L	O	H	W	D
N	U	O	S	Q	V	P	I	T	Z	L	S	N	D	B	T	I	S	O
S	O	O	J	H	Y	E	W	Q	L	N	I	F	L	M	C	T	I	R
X	W	T	Y	Z	N	O	L	I	U	L	Y	M	E	E	X	P	D	P
S	P	Q	S	M	P	D	K	G	B	R	O	H	X	H	W	E	V	E
P	E	N	C	D	G	D	E	R	D	N	I	K	S	N	A	H	D	H
H	U	H	S	O	A	Z	T	Q	X	B	O	Z	D	L	S	X	W	T

Download Festival 2007

Across

4. The apparatus for executing the sentence of death by hanging. (7)

6. Father bug. (4, 5)

9. Formed by Nikki and Tommy in 1981. (6, 4)

11. The unforgiving dutch symphonic metal band. (6, 10)

14. Satans chauffeur. (11)

15. Silky handgun. (6, 8)

Down

1. Phineas and Ferbs experiment Blows Up Roofing. (7, 3, 4)

2. Operate emergency stop button. (10, 6)

3. Formed on Christmas Day 1975 by Steve Harris. (4, 6)

5. Flower Moth lays a cosmic egg. (10)

7. Every question needs this. (3, 6)

8. Another word for creators, designers or devisers. (10)

10. Twice nominated for best metal performance grammy award with singles Get inside and Inhale. (5,4)

12. Hillbilly rock band. (7,5)

13. An american prog metal band named after their local venue. (5, 7)

Download Festival 2007

See if you can find the acts from Download 2007 in the word search below. It is tricky though, words can be in any direction in a straight line, front or backward.

N	M	O	T	L	E	Y	C	R	U	E	Q	Y	U	Q	B	K	T	R
S	H	V	K	A	S	P	G	A	U	B	L	V	Z	T	O	S	R	E
G	I	J	R	E	H	T	O	M	F	L	O	W	Z	P	S	V	T	J
E	H	W	S	P	W	P	A	P	A	R	O	A	C	H	N	G	M	O
R	Q	X	W	Z	D	E	V	I	L	D	R	I	V	E	R	Q	Z	T
T	C	P	C	P	U	O	S	R	O	F	G	N	I	L	W	O	B	C
A	K	I	L	L	S	W	I	T	C	H	E	N	G	A	G	E	Z	T
E	J	B	D	T	R	E	V	L	O	V	E	R	T	E	V	L	E	V
H	Z	W	I	T	H	I	N	T	E	M	P	T	A	T	I	O	N	A
T	H	N	H	C	D	E	Y	C	N	O	E	E	G	V	C	M	Z	P
M	F	E	S	T	I	X	A	Z	S	T	C	E	T	I	H	C	R	A
A	K	D	E	B	G	W	E	N	Z	N	P	D	T	N	J	Q	S	G
E	F	I	K	H	I	Y	L	K	S	S	W	O	L	L	A	G	N	E
R	O	A	Z	Q	X	P	F	F	L	W	W	N	V	M	Q	L	I	Y
D	F	M	H	H	F	O	A	Z	M	F	E	Z	D	N	J	L	A	H
A	J	N	B	T	V	W	C	M	S	I	W	R	C	S	B	N	U	P
D	K	O	R	U	O	S	E	N	O	T	S	P	M	J	K	K	S	P
S	Y	R	P	A	H	V	W	R	L	K	B	E	U	S	R	H	Q	T
B	W	I	R	C	D	H	A	Y	S	E	E	D	D	I	X	I	E	O

Download Festival 2008

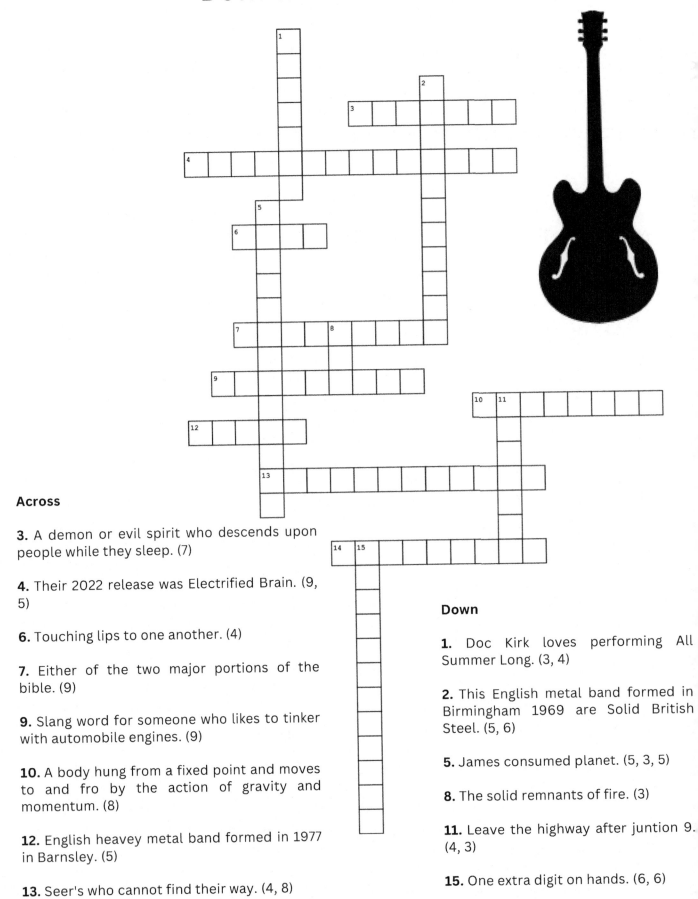

Across

3. A demon or evil spirit who descends upon people while they sleep. (7)

4. Their 2022 release was Electrified Brain. (9, 5)

6. Touching lips to one another. (4)

7. Either of the two major portions of the bible. (9)

9. Slang word for someone who likes to tinker with automobile engines. (9)

10. A body hung from a fixed point and moves to and fro by the action of gravity and momentum. (8)

12. English heavey metal band formed in 1977 in Barnsley. (5)

13. Seer's who cannot find their way. (4, 8)

14. A pretty fly californian punk rock band. (9)

Down

1. Doc Kirk loves performing All Summer Long. (3, 4)

2. This English metal band formed in Birmingham 1969 are Solid British Steel. (5, 6)

5. James consumed planet. (5, 3, 5)

8. The solid remnants of fire. (3)

11. Leave the highway after juntion 9. (4, 3)

15. One extra digit on hands. (6, 6)

Download Festival 2008

See if you can find the acts from Download 2008 in the word search below. It is tricky though, words can be in any direction in a straight line, front or backward.

X	M	Z	L	C	A	Y	R	A	L	S	U	B	U	C	N	I	A	D
Z	O	M	L	E	B	N	P	W	H	I	E	Z	U	X	K	K	R	A
S	Y	D	Y	F	L	G	L	H	I	H	N	P	N	M	I	J	K	R
A	F	K	T	K	M	M	P	N	H	A	E	J	J	U	I	C	W	A
U	X	L	A	J	K	T	L	G	X	O	V	I	M	N	P	Y	G	I
W	W	G	S	V	C	M	H	F	N	F	E	M	T	I	G	C	V	L
Z	C	P	E	N	D	U	L	U	M	F	L	M	E	C	J	E	D	A
S	U	O	A	R	F	I	H	X	P	S	E	Y	S	I	U	X	A	S
A	Q	T	S	T	V	L	M	P	R	P	R	E	T	P	D	I	E	I
X	V	S	H	J	N	U	M	C	T	R	E	A	A	A	A	T	H	S
O	Q	X	M	T	K	N	K	L	G	I	G	T	M	L	S	T	R	I
N	S	W	I	V	E	C	C	N	L	N	N	W	E	W	P	E	O	R
I	Z	Z	G	T	X	Y	O	D	O	G	I	O	N	A	R	N	T	O
Q	W	O	S	G	Y	Q	D	R	C	R	F	R	T	S	I	A	O	B
P	V	E	P	S	U	C	Q	M	D	N	X	L	D	T	E	R	M	O
Q	W	M	O	W	I	Z	Z	A	E	I	D	D	T	E	S	P	O	M
H	Z	F	D	G	E	K	R	M	U	L	K	Q	R	J	T	W	W	R
O	Z	K	R	L	O	S	T	P	R	O	P	H	E	T	S	K	K	C
T	M	U	H	D	I	D	M	M	P	E	F	V	M	X	X	B	R	A

Download Festival 2009

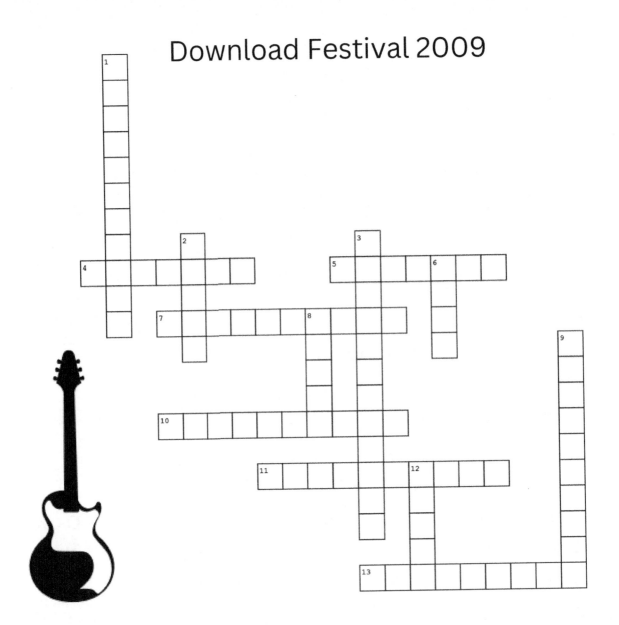

Across

4. Don't stop believing. (7)

5. Always accompanies lightning. (7)

7. What you get if you dunk your digestive too long. (4, 6)

10. Hard of hearing big cat. (3, 7)

11. Both of us at half a dozen. (3, 2, 2, 3)

13. A region of spacetime where gravity is so strong nothing can escape. (9)

Down

1. What a holy man has who no longer believes. (5, 2, 4)

2. A large block of metal with a flattened top. (5)

3. Primary lyricist and singer for Sound Garden. (5, 7)

6. Opposite to up. (4)

8. These are very Sharp Dressed Men with fine beards. (2, 3)

9. Well known band with hits including Here I Go Again and Is This Love. (10)

12. This bands namesake was known for his contributions to the modern alternating current electricity supply. (5)

Download Festival 2009

ee if you can find the acts from Download 2009 in the
ord search below. It is tricky though, words can be in
any direction in a straight line, front or backward.

B	R	O	U	D	H	M	O	M	Z	B	Q	B	L	G	N	O	V	X
Q	K	Y	K	H	E	N	D	O	W	N	R	L	J	C	K	A	N	E
J	V	O	H	I	E	F	M	I	J	H	E	J	D	Q	A	Z	J	T
K	U	U	P	R	H	N	L	X	H	R	M	W	U	B	H	K	T	E
R	X	M	I	Y	F	U	U	E	O	H	H	R	L	G	G	B	K	S
B	E	E	W	M	B	A	X	M	P	I	U	A	E	D	S	H	H	L
F	H	A	W	Z	H	F	O	C	T	P	C	R	A	D	Y	V	B	A
P	I	T	C	O	Y	N	P	E	A	K	A	R	F	R	N	H	H	F
V	U	S	U	R	H	S	S	A	H	N	D	R	J	Y	F	U	M	B
P	I	I	N	T	G	N	X	O	G	Q	V	H	D	A	M	O	H	V
G	T	X	I	W	A	E	L	E	P	X	K	I	Z	J	Q	H	Z	T
M	I	A	G	K	F	E	A	O	X	K	V	X	L	C	L	Y	O	V
G	F	J	E	E	O	V	T	T	I	K	Z	I	B	P	M	I	L	H
Z	G	Z	R	U	O	Z	G	G	G	F	P	H	H	G	P	W	H	F
X	C	S	V	H	Z	N	N	P	E	D	P	X	W	S	B	L	K	N
I	Z	G	A	V	X	X	W	J	O	U	R	N	E	Y	E	D	Q	C
D	L	R	Q	E	J	G	Q	Y	Q	S	Z	E	L	L	C	S	S	T
E	I	B	D	L	B	O	R	I	S	I	S	A	L	I	A	R	E	Q
W	V	Y	Y	Y	C	H	R	I	S	C	O	R	N	E	L	L	R	R

Download Festival 2010

Across

2. Lead singer for a band with a smelly name. (4)

4. This band collaborated with rap group Run DMC in 1986. (9)

7. A stripy animals uppermost part of its body. (9)

8. Siblings Lizzy and Arejay named this band after their last name and inclement weather. (9)

9. A vibrant, multicultural district in the east end of London. (11)

10. British progressive rock band who released their 11th album, closure/continuation, in June 2022 after a 13 year gap. (9, 4)

11. Alternating current and direct. (4)

12. You shall go to the ball. (10)

Down

1. This bands debut album, Core, released in reached number 3 in the US charts. (5, 6, 6)

2. Glam metal parody band. (5, 7)

3. A radio frequency. (2)

5. Those wonky scavenger birds. (4, 7, 8)

6. A Danish metal band. (7)

Download Festival 2010

ee if you can find the acts from Download 2010 in the word search below. It is tricky though, words can be in any direction in a straight line, front or backward.

T	Q	Z	K	B	Q	S	N	V	C	Z	T	J	B	D	C	I	K	T
E	Z	I	N	I	K	S	C	I	O	F	T	T	U	A	T	C	Z	H
O	S	C	M	G	B	X	F	C	Z	L	R	S	X	U	O	Y	S	E
D	R	G	M	D	C	X	L	F	I	E	B	F	V	B	R	J	T	M
A	P	S	U	R	B	N	U	M	H	W	O	E	C	V	A	U	O	C
E	G	F	B	M	O	X	U	T	C	I	C	S	A	X	I	E	L	R
H	E	X	J	Y	E	T	N	Z	T	B	B	T	K	T	L	Z	I	O
A	E	H	G	E	U	A	S	E	A	L	D	E	P	A	A	P	P	O
R	S	R	E	B	P	E	U	E	L	E	T	C	D	E	S	B	E	K
B	X	X	R	L	U	H	D	T	L	P	B	G	N	R	I	L	L	E
E	X	N	E	O	B	G	X	V	E	A	Z	E	X	O	S	S	P	D
Z	N	E	U	E	E	R	B	F	R	H	H	N	W	S	I	R	M	V
E	T	T	F	R	F	U	B	V	E	C	N	K	N	M	R	J	E	U
S	O	D	C	M	K	D	O	P	D	E	P	U	X	I	O	N	T	L
Y	Z	N	D	S	A	V	U	P	N	T	B	I	U	T	B	P	E	T
P	P	Q	C	O	P	D	A	J	I	I	R	V	T	H	O	B	N	U
N	S	S	A	S	L	S	B	L	C	H	G	J	V	J	P	Z	O	R
T	A	V	M	C	X	E	U	U	X	W	J	X	G	T	C	P	T	E
I	G	R	D	P	O	R	C	U	P	I	N	E	T	R	E	E	S	S

Download Festival 2011

Across

4. To steal from an undead reanimated corpse. (3, 6)

7. A group held together by a shared commitment to a charismatic leader or ideology. (3, 4)

9. The title of a 1990 romantic fantasy film starring Demi Moore but I doubt this satanic band had that in mind when choosing their name. (5)

12. Loss of hearing in Cuban capital city. (4, 6)

13. This bands lead singer is called Skin. (5, 7)

15. Bent out of shape sibling. (7, 6)

Down

1. Poor Cecelia. (5, 6)

2. Skinny Elizabeth (4, 5)

3. This Armenian-American band encouraged people to steal their 2002 album. (6, 2, 1, 4)

5. This band took their name from a track on the 1970 Free album, Fire and Water. (2, 3)

6. This band could pose a threat to the health of living organisms, primarily that of humans. (9)

8. This bands biggest hit was Hey There Dililah. (5, 5, 2)

10. A form of giving insults usually found in sports. (5, 4)

11. They let her Pick Her Act and she announced Tonight Its You. (5, 5)

14. This English singer songwriter believes in writing Positive Songs For Negative People. (5, 6)

Download Festival 2011

ee if you can find the acts from Download 2011 in the
word search below. It is tricky though, words can be in
any direction in a straight line, front or backward.

```
S  T  P  W  D  X  A  V  B  C  Y  B  D  F  J  L  Q  H  L
T  W  R  W  F  E  Y  T  I  G  D  Z  F  L  H  F  T  P  V
E  I  S  N  A  N  A  K  N  U  K  S  Z  C  V  I  X  D  D
T  S  U  C  Z  L  D  F  D  R  O  M  N  I  E  K  S  R  B
I  T  A  T  C  O  I  W  H  P  Y  L  B  Q  L  Y  E  A  U
H  E  K  H  Z  N  T  C  M  A  C  S  E  V  S  N  U  Z  Y
W  D  Z  H  T  F  K  W  E  Z  V  I  M  T  Q  C  I  A  J
N  S  R  B  X  M  R  R  V  C  B  A  E  R  H  J  I  H  J
I  I  M  T  H  T  Q  A  E  M  O  M  N  E  S  H  I  O  T
A  S  O  Y  A  V  A  B  O  N  O  O  A  A  T  U  T  I  R
L  T  A  W  K  K  Z  Z  M  F  R  P  P  S  P  S  X  B  C
P  E  F  M  K  N  B  Z  A  J  T  U  O  E  W  K  S  G  H
K  R  O  U  A  O  E  D  D  R  N  H  T  V  R  L  W  X  Z
G  U  Y  K  R  Z  O  I  I  N  G  H  I  K  J  Y  V  Q  C
G  I  B  R  M  W  T  C  H  X  Q  S  V  C  N  L  Q  K  L
G  G  G  G  N  R  K  P  T  T  R  A  S  H  T  A  L  K  V
X  B  Y  U  R  A  C  F  C  K  Y  C  N  X  Z  N  R  N  E
U  I  G  X  Z  V  Y  W  H  U  Q  N  Q  T  Y  O  F  F  E
W  W  S  I  N  T  H  E  C  U  L  T  P  F  N  K  Q  G  D
```

Download Festival 2012

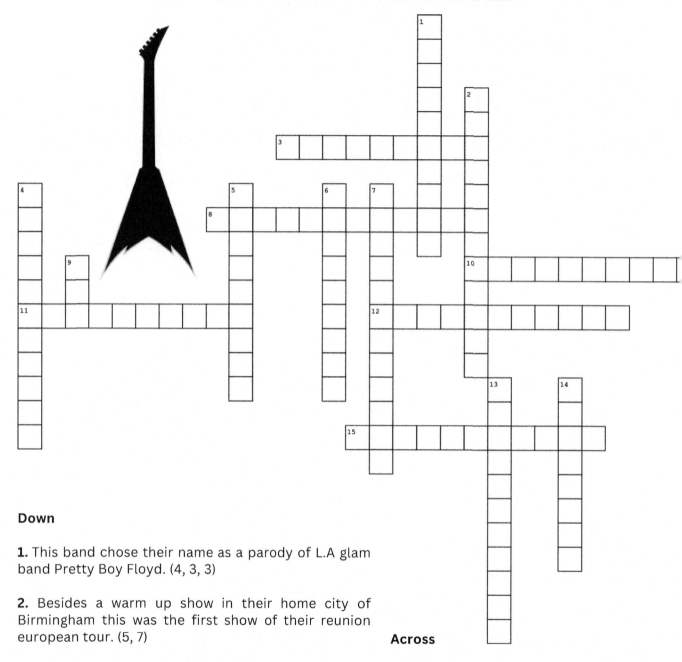

Down

1. This band chose their name as a parody of L.A glam band Pretty Boy Floyd. (4, 3, 3)

2. Besides a warm up show in their home city of Birmingham this was the first show of their reunion european tour. (5, 7)

4. This band took their name from a character from Hard Core Logo. (5, 6)

5. This band were given a Second Chance, but not the last, to play Download. (9)

6. Competing siblings. (5, 4)

7. This bands biggest hit was Tequila. (12)

9. An instrument of death. (3)

13. Where terror is manufactured. (4, 7)

14. Super metal group formed in 2012 with a debut album called Vultures. (8)

Across

3. Performed their legendary black album. (9)

8. This band originally called themselves The Queerboys but decided on a mInoR change (3, 9)

10. This band won best album at the 2014 Kerrang! awards with Opposites. (5, 5)

11. A comedy rock duo who pay tribute to the greatest song in the world. (9, 1)

12. Stand up in opposition. (4, 7)

15. Blackhole sun is considered this band signature song. (11)

Download Festival 2012

ee if you can find the acts from Download 2012 in the word search below. It is tricky though, words can be in any direction in a straight line, front or backward.

```
B  Z  E  R  I  V  A  L  S  O  N  S  C  T  E  G  N  N  F
N  L  Y  O  Y  Q  D  K  K  X  Y  Q  E  B  S  U  J  C  P
O  T  A  M  J  D  O  F  L  W  J  N  C  Y  O  N  Y  U  M
I  F  M  C  R  D  R  R  B  K  A  X  O  M  M  P  I  T  B
S  D  E  R  K  P  I  I  Y  C  V  B  O  C  R  S  M  A  A
I  Q  T  A  J  S  Z  K  I  L  E  I  K  A  M  Y  W  G  K
V  T  A  O  R  G  A  O  Y  R  C  X  L  H  Z  J  C  F  D
R  Y  L  B  V  F  U  B  I  L  L  Y  T  A  L  E  N  T  N
O  L  L  Z  O  S  A  U  B  W  G  D  F  X  G  G  A  K  W
R  B  I  A  D  R  Q  C  Z  A  N  U  F  F  P  M  R  V  O
R  X  C  D  I  E  I  F  T  U  T  V  F  Q  I  O  V  A  D
E  W  A  G  H  Q  E  S  O  O  Z  H  H  Y  N  B  U  U  E
T  I  G  T  Y  N  Z  W  I  Q  R  L  L  D  V  W  U  H  N
O  B  T  M  O  Z  E  G  C  S  K  Y  G  U  O  W  D  S  I
U  O  Z  C  O  X  N  E  D  R  A  G  D  N  U  O  S  R  H
T  S  N  I  A  G  A  E  S  I  R  L  C  B  X  U  U  W  S
T  X  N  T  T  L  L  L  X  Y  Q  W  I  N  M  V  M  I  Y
L  K  R  J  C  L  Y  Y  J  D  J  E  A  A  D  E  N  Z  W
Y  P  Q  Q  D  H  R  O  N  H  N  H  B  J  R  Z  Q  S  E
```

Download Festival 2013

Across

3. Entomb the next day. (4, 8)

6. Took their name from a misprinted label of Black Sabbaths third album. (7, 2, 7)

8. Unidentified Flying Object. (3)

10. An australian rock band who have been Runnin' Wild since 2003. (9)

13. A memorable time. (1, 3, 2, 8)

Down

1. The dead centre of any town. (9)

2. This band thought about Pneumonia Hawk for name but decided on a different combination illness and animal. (6, 4)

4. This german bands name literally translates Ramming Stone. (9)

5. A swedish metal band not to be confused with welsh rock band. (9)

7. What goes up must come .... (4)

9. A female ruler. (7)

11. This band is still going strong after more th 50 years but its only original member is Mick B on guitar. (5, 4)

12. This band are perhaps best known for the song, The Final Countdown'. (6)

Download Festival 2013

ee if you can find the acts from Download 2013 in the
vord search below. It is tricky though, words can be in
any direction in a straight line, front or backward.

```
U  N  K  V  R  E  I  K  D  W  A  W  P  Z  Z  C  H  M  S
P  S  Y  Q  U  O  I  A  H  I  O  N  X  S  L  D  Y  A  S
G  F  F  R  Y  F  R  F  N  R  Q  S  H  M  B  T  J  S  E
U  Y  O  L  E  U  A  O  R  A  M  M  S  T  E  I  N  T  R
Y  P  O  I  A  B  T  O  K  A  C  N  Q  N  O  E  Q  E  P
E  X  E  E  Y  A  M  M  W  A  V  Z  Y  Q  P  D  W  R  M
S  L  L  A  T  O  Y  E  N  A  O  S  N  M  Q  P  P  S  E
W  W  Z  A  T  O  A  C  M  X  G  T  L  E  P  J  B  O  Z
R  P  K  Y  W  L  E  I  W  E  A  V  M  O  G  P  L  F  K
Y  H  R  E  J  R  W  N  R  B  R  J  R  C  D  O  P  R  T
E  U  I  B  B  N  P  Y  Q  B  F  O  P  P  V  Z  K  E  P
B  X  V  A  P  S  K  J  H  C  O  D  T  E  X  K  L  A  W
U  O  T  P  E  E  H  H  A  I  R  U  N  Y  B  I  I  L  M
A  S  G  M  P  M  C  Y  S  H  W  H  R  W  A  E  S  I  O
B  O  R  I  S  I  S  A  L  I  A  R  H  N  O  D  K  T  E
D  R  A  Y  E  V  A  R  G  Y  X  V  Q  R  E  D  A  Y  H
R  C  P  N  Q  F  C  W  V  M  C  D  Q  E  A  B  E  N  K
E  G  O  F  N  W  Z  A  Q  N  I  F  B  N  X  T  Q  B  F
L  A  T  I  F  Z  X  Z  O  R  J  M  F  I  S  V  K  Y  K
```

Download Festival 2014

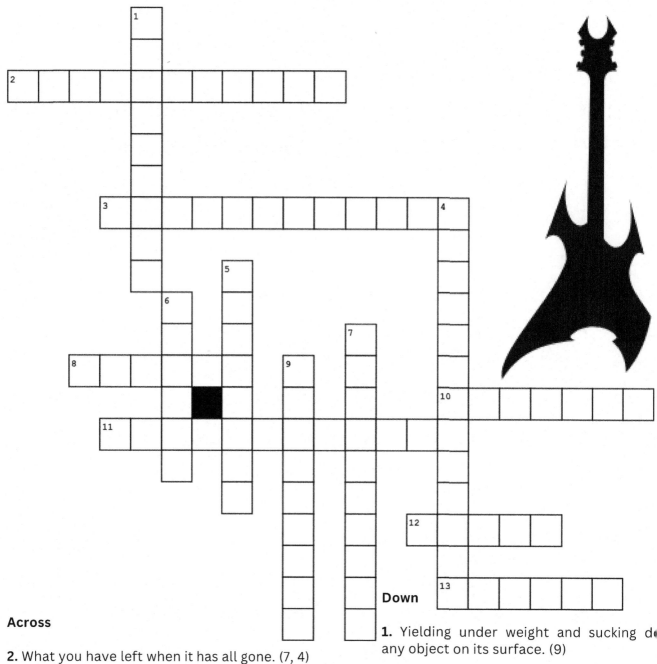

Across

2. What you have left when it has all gone. (7, 4)

3. So dangerous it is worth repeating twice. (6, 6)

8. A band from Sheffield consisting of two Loveless brothers. (6)

10. An american christian rock band formed in 1996. (7)

11. "Samoa Banjoes" are excellent for playing blues rock. (3, 9)

12. A metal band fronted by a professional wrestler. (5)

13. An electronic image that represents and may be manipulated by a computer user. (6)

Down

1. Yielding under weight and sucking d⟨ any object on its surface. (9)

4. Best known for having once been the ⟨ guitarist for a famous New Jersey band. (6

5. A huge and monsterous polish death m⟨ band. (8)

6. In certain sports, such as football or ru⟨ this is a players position on either outer e⟨ of the field. (6)

7. Regal stuff flowing through those veins. (5, 5)

9. This band have been Rockin' all over World in their 60 plus years of playing. (6,

Download Festival 2014

See if you can find the acts from Download 2014 in the word search below. It is tricky though, words can be in any direction in a straight line, front or backward.

```
R  J  Q  A  W  L  W  D  O  D  C  E  T  X  S  T  A  J  R
A  U  X  P  G  E  S  L  O  X  R  J  B  L  X  L  W  A  B
E  R  D  S  M  M  Q  B  D  O  W  E  L  G  A  C  T  R  O
Z  N  E  Y  D  D  B  H  E  N  L  A  N  O  O  A  C  O  R
I  O  L  C  N  T  M  I  T  L  P  B  Q  G  V  C  Z  B  I
R  E  G  N  A  D  R  E  G  N  A  D  L  A  E  S  T  M  S
B  T  M  H  S  B  E  H  E  M  O  T  H  A  J  C  Y  A  I
E  X  I  M  K  I  F  S  E  B  W  N  U  O  Y  M  X  S  S
U  N  G  V  C  O  O  R  I  Z  B  I  E  B  T  O  N  E  A
R  N  D  L  I  F  Q  B  O  X  F  B  N  M  J  T  R  I  L
S  Q  O  W  U  B  B  U  Q  A  O  W  N  G  U  X  U  H  I
F  I  L  B  Q  U  T  I  W  N  Z  I  J  Y  E  S  O  C  A
N  S  J  P  O  E  C  B  A  E  Z  Q  H  O  B  R  T  I  R
S  B  T  X  L  F  U  M  I  Q  Y  C  C  M  U  B  K  R  W
M  U  H  L  Y  N  A  E  R  O  M  G  N  I  H  T  O  N  K
E  V  I  K  I  S  S  T  A  T  U  S  Q  U  O  Q  F  V  H
P  K  U  H  S  U  L  C  G  S  J  Z  F  T  A  T  W  Q  O
S  G  N  A  J  N  N  H  X  X  O  K  G  H  Y  O  W  J  V
T  T  A  Z  G  R  A  V  B  E  Y  P  Q  S  W  Q  M  W  A
```

Download Festival 2015

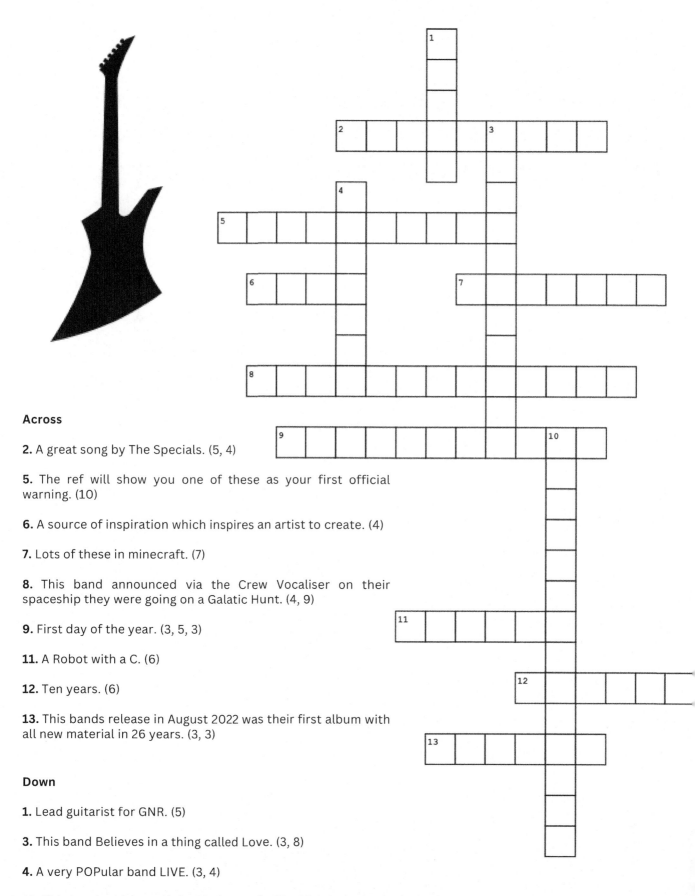

Across

2. A great song by The Specials. (5, 4)

5. The ref will show you one of these as your first official warning. (10)

6. A source of inspiration which inspires an artist to create. (4)

7. Lots of these in minecraft. (7)

8. This band announced via the Crew Vocaliser on their spaceship they were going on a Galatic Hunt. (4, 9)

9. First day of the year. (3, 5, 3)

11. A Robot with a C. (6)

12. Ten years. (6)

13. This bands release in August 2022 was their first album with all new material in 26 years. (3, 3)

Down

1. Lead guitarist for GNR. (5)

3. This band Believes in a thing called Love. (3, 8)

4. A very POPular band LIVE. (3, 4)

10. This band understand the Madness of a War You Cannot Win. (3, 4, 7)

Download Festival 2015

ee if you can find the acts from Download 2015 in the
word search below. It is tricky though, words can be in
any direction in a straight line, front or backward.

```
L  I  D  A  E  O  N  T  F  Y  O  Q  C  R  E  E  B  K  Y
P  J  F  E  J  O  O  W  O  J  M  I  A  E  X  V  O  N  S
H  U  Z  M  S  B  Z  W  O  K  Z  B  X  P  Z  I  R  J  I
U  H  U  C  O  O  V  U  G  T  M  I  K  E  X  L  I  T  C
L  S  P  R  D  E  C  A  D  E  T  F  E  E  H  S  S  M  M
E  M  C  L  Y  U  X  Z  B  V  H  S  U  R  Q  C  I  X  I
Y  A  D  S  R  A  E  Y  W  E  N  Q  O  C  C  A  S  G  X
Z  L  T  H  E  D  A  R  K  N  E  S  S  H  N  R  A  H  G
S  N  I  A  M  E  R  T  A  H  T  L  L  A  G  E  L  U  V
Z  V  L  V  D  O  I  U  P  Y  Z  L  U  B  Q  C  I  X  J
J  T  Y  T  E  U  J  T  I  F  E  X  R  O  P  R  A  K  O
I  H  U  C  T  P  B  N  D  V  H  L  P  N  J  O  R  Z  Q
F  C  V  U  G  H  O  W  A  I  S  N  L  Q  H  W  I  Y  S
W  G  G  V  T  T  V  P  A  W  A  P  A  O  C  R  J  N  T
K  Q  M  D  E  A  Z  V  P  R  L  B  B  I  W  L  F  F  D
A  H  X  P  B  C  P  C  B  K  S  X  W  A  W  C  O  O  S
L  L  N  W  V  C  X  G  V  W  H  A  D  J  E  H  A  E  D
K  O  A  A  Y  N  D  N  W  R  I  V  O  N  O  E  M  R  D
T  Z  G  R  U  V  R  R  Y  A  I  K  I  Z  V  U  K  B  D
```

Download Festival 2016

Across

6. Shameful or disgraceful Until I Die. (10)

8. She has Been Caught Stealing. (5, 9)

9. A crystalline cube shaped container vessel for the space stone. (9)

11. This band has headlined more times at Download than any other band. (4, 6)

12. An expression of surprise or frustration after having to change their name from Baby Godzilla after a lawsuit with a Japanese film company. (4)

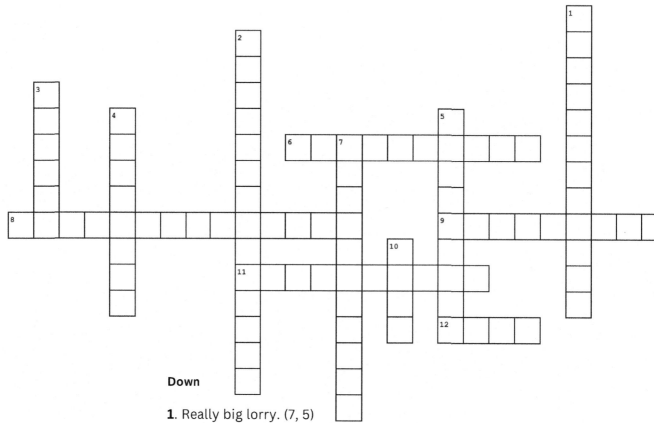

Down

1. Really big lorry. (7, 5)

2. This English doom metal band took their name from two Black Sabbat song titles. (8, 6)

3. The Hun. (6)

4. A fighters vulnerability were one is easily knocked out by a blow to th chin. (8)

5. These usually fall out between 3 and 6 years. (4, 5)

7. This 3 piece metal band from Stockholm released their self titled album i 2001. (5, 6)

10. This band has headlined three times at download. (4)

Download Festival 2016

See if you can find the acts from Download 2016 in the word search below. It is tricky though, words can be in any direction in a straight line, front or backward.

```
Q E V E X E E A R P V Y S C E B N K S
X I L K A F J T Y G M B Q H S H R R U
S D C E T B E T K Y J H F G B T A I N
D E M T C F X I C O Q G T O O D O C G
H B N W Z T Y L S U O I R O L G N I A
G O P Z N Z R A Q T H I O N H Y D M M
Q B R R O Z M I E X S P O A O I M I D
L P Q W A H S S C I W I D B Z F C L N
T Q V D D M S R S W T A M H X Y Z K A
O D E M X E I A R C I I J E R V P T R
K I S S R L L R I N I Z I S C E I E G
Y S H A B I U D O E C F A T S L J E G
S P C I A K D E X N C C E R J A L T W
V T Y R L A L D K R M E R P D Q L H J
P R C P S W H H P G V A H W O F E G W
A Q P E D Q K T J J H N I X S Z W D X
M O N S T E R T R U C K D D U A L Z U
K A U Q E Z N U D U C Y I C E I I T Y
J I C E Y T P S X T F J H X U N M S Q
```

Download Festival 2017

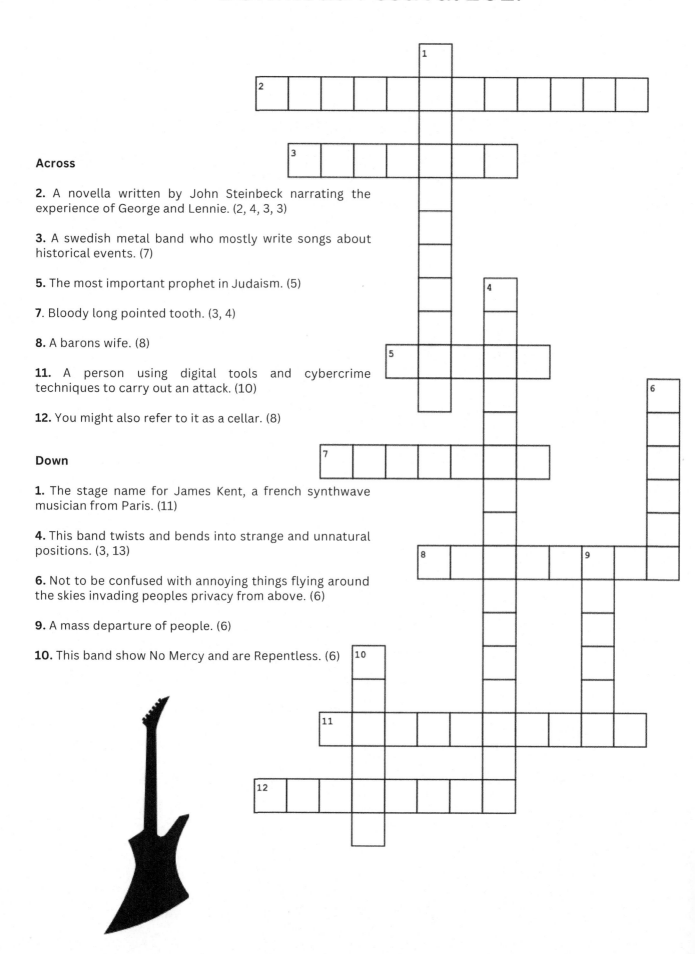

Across

2. A novella written by John Steinbeck narrating the experience of George and Lennie. (2, 4, 3, 3)

3. A swedish metal band who mostly write songs about historical events. (7)

5. The most important prophet in Judaism. (5)

7. Bloody long pointed tooth. (3, 4)

8. A barons wife. (8)

11. A person using digital tools and cybercrime techniques to carry out an attack. (10)

12. You might also refer to it as a cellar. (8)

Down

1. The stage name for James Kent, a french synthwave musician from Paris. (11)

4. This band twists and bends into strange and unnatural positions. (3, 13)

6. Not to be confused with annoying things flying around the skies invading peoples privacy from above. (6)

9. A mass departure of people. (6)

10. This band show No Mercy and are Repentless. (6)

Download Festival 2017

See if you can find the acts from Download 2017 in the word search below. It is tricky though, words can be in any direction in a straight line, front or backward.

```
F  W  M  S  R  R  V  O  K  F  R  O  N  L  N  T  K  A  H
V  W  Y  R  P  E  O  I  H  E  I  E  X  J  B  S  W  G  D
K  A  T  U  X  C  W  T  D  S  M  Z  R  F  C  I  D  H  V
E  A  K  O  V  R  T  F  A  D  B  J  A  M  O  V  Z  I  C
E  S  D  I  W  R  A  C  N  B  M  E  Z  Y  E  I  Q  E  E
W  U  J  S  L  N  H  A  W  E  R  H  B  R  G  T  W  F  Z
S  F  O  W  G  L  E  L  A  Q  C  U  S  B  V  K  S  N  J
S  A  J  J  B  C  M  O  S  E  S  N  T  O  J  C  D  V  D
S  S  P  C  I  H  N  M  L  C  O  T  F  R  Y  A  E  N  Z
T  P  E  M  M  W  R  W  N  M  S  U  M  A  E  H  C  O  J
V  A  F  N  G  U  L  S  N  Q  E  G  W  I  J  P  N  E  S
P  O  E  Y  O  N  M  D  I  K  L  U  S  F  M  X  O  O  B
D  O  L  H  V  R  R  D  V  S  W  S  O  Z  M  X  T  S  G
Y  R  T  H  C  I  A  S  C  H  G  C  I  B  L  J  A  L  E
R  T  O  I  F  U  Z  B  A  W  U  A  K  H  T  W  B  A  N
T  S  I  N  O  I  T  R  O  T  N  O  C  E  H  T  A  Y  F
T  N  E  M  E  S  A  B  O  Z  L  Q  W  T  F  O  S  E  G
L  C  E  H  P  S  B  O  R  I  S  I  S  A  L  I  A  R  I
H  J  Y  B  D  S  J  H  I  T  Q  B  I  A  J  S  S  D  J
```

Download Festival 2018

Across

3. Something people might race for in the states. (3, 4, 5)

4. You cannot hate this band from Liverpool or The Things They Believe. (6)

7. Expensive item for opening locks in a Mechanical World. (4, 3)

10. A procession on the first monday of May. (6, 6)

11. This band want you to refuse to change your beliefs. (5, 2, 4, 4)

13. The one and only Prince of Darkness. (4, 8)

Down

1. Baby dog. (5)

2. Lead singer of an iconic nu metal band, not to be confused with the welsh rugby union player. (8, 5)

5. Everybody wants this Young and Dangerous group even in these Strange Days. (3, 6)

6. A term used sometimes to refer to a supreme being (6, 5)

8. A borough of New York City known for the Yankee Stadium. (3, 5)

9. This welsh pop punk band with have you buried sand up to your head. (4, 4)

12. This band are notorious for keeping audience waiting. (4, 1, 5)

Download Festival 2018

See if you can find the acts from Download 2018 in the word search below. It is tricky though, words can be in any direction in a straight line, front or backward.

```
L E L G P U P P Y O E I Q V O H S L R
F M D Y U N U T O K D E O O Q V N W E
S I V A D N O H T A N O J R Q L U T W
R P X K R A S D Y R G C R R K T G H O
Z N B F T A Z N U F H F I M H O R E P
P I Q X Y P P O R D E H Y E N I U S R
L R M J L Z B Y V O L H P E P D O T E
B W H A D S A X A F S I T M O K Y R H
U O B S O J N R Z D N E N A Y V O U G
X K R Y U O X S D K Y D S C O S T T I
R W Z I R M R T S D I A N D N L K S H
G Z X B S G O L D K E Y M V U O C G W
O Y E U H I I P E E D K C E N K I Z H
A H Q D F P S O U U Q A P C C W T T U
T A D R S I T A U J S U U C C G S E V
G E W D J J K F L N T X W X Z W A S C
L I J R Z M M S F I D Z F X H P H B L
V A M B Q X V P V P A E A Z O P P J L
C Q X I Y N G L H P T R V T H Q K C L
```

Download Festival 2019

Across

3. People tend to get this after a few too many drinks. (7, 6)

6. When this bands album sold over 10,000,000 copies they surely did not feel Mellon Collie and Infinitely Sad. (8, 8)

8. This Swedish melodic death metal band take their name from the Sinderin name of Mount Doom, a volcano in J.R.R Tolkiens middle earth. (4, 6)

9. A dead body. (7)

10. This band formed in Tokyo and took their name from a Halestorm song they played in rehearsals. (9)

11. You also get a lot of this in the U.K thanks to 9 down. (8)

Down

1. Hello July (7, 4)

2. This Welsh band played Download three times o the weekend. (5, 4, 5)

4. At the end of the queue. (4, 2, 4)

5. A neighbourhood in Downtown Los Angeles offici known as Central East City. (4, 3)

7. Elvis fronted Nirvana cover band. (6)

9. You see them in the sky a lot in the U.K. (5)

Download Festival 2019

ee if you can find the acts from Download 2019 in the
ord search below. It is tricky though, words can be in
any direction in a straight line, front or backward.

```
S M A S H I N G P U M P K I N S S L E
P Z X X Z F P N D J B F L J K S W A L
G L B J C O Q O M V P Z N I A T C S V
M R J Q U T H M E D H Q D C H O C T A
E N U J E Y B D O O G R R K L L U I N
S W B F S R I Y L U O A C D E V A N A
D W B D O P Z D X W C L R L V I A L Z
D U O O F D C F A A U A H X O E C I A
H N U R R M C G E I I W T G L U S N C
B L K I C I J Q C N L K R K F T D E Z
W N Q Y S N S D Q Q G W A M U W Q A H
H L G Z U G M I C C B M M O K H N M A
V T T O Z N L A S Q L Z A J F C B T S
Z P B C F E O K D A M H N W X W C T Y
L O V E B I T E S E L W O W U D L C E
H X S H L U L G M Y S I M K J E F N R
P P H Z Y O A X Q U Y O A W W B Q O P
E H G K M L N N G P P W H R U L O R W
N O I S I V D E R R U L B T R B A R T
```

Download Festival 2021

Across

2. Baby tiger. (7)

4. Everyone likes a nice glass of this before bed, especially children. (3, 4)

5. This lead singer left Reuben to become the King of Clubs. (5, 6)

7. The opposite of benevolent. (11)

9. Stop us if you've heard Death Whistler. (3, 10)

Down

1. This band loves a good a Curry. (7, 6)

3. It Ain't Always Easy but this band have been a Revelation. (5, 6)

6. You could say waiters and butlers are recruited for this. (8, 2, 5)

8. British punk rock band who named themselves after an episode of the Regular Show when Rigby changed his name. (5, 4)

Download Festival 2021

See if you can find the acts from Download 2021 in the word search below. It is tricky though, words can be in any direction in a straight line, front or backward.

```
T  T  E  E  D  I  A  H  Z  P  D  J  B  T  C  Q  E  O  F
S  D  W  P  C  D  V  U  D  S  J  N  U  R  I  E  M  L  S
D  J  L  A  E  N  I  R  D  V  E  C  C  A  M  W  C  Z  T
V  E  A  R  Z  V  E  X  V  K  Y  M  R  S  V  R  J  G  R
K  L  I  M  T  O  H  L  O  K  Y  J  E  H  S  I  U  X  A
C  B  Q  G  I  A  H  R  O  D  P  U  G  B  F  F  A  M  E
M  M  P  A  V  E  B  F  E  V  C  Q  I  O  U  Y  B  S  H
Q  P  N  B  L  E  L  V  E  Y  E  B  T  A  G  F  A  Q  D
C  O  T  F  N  Z  E  E  F  O  F  L  O  T  W  N  F  Q  L
Z  Y  Y  O  T  Q  T  O  N  W  U  G  A  X  E  E  R  I  I
X  V  T  H  O  A  Q  F  W  M  E  W  P  M  M  P  D  D  W
I  S  M  A  S  S  I  V  E  W  A  G  O  N  S  R  U  L  E
X  H  D  A  K  Z  U  B  V  S  P  N  H  W  S  O  I  X  H
E  V  R  E  S  O  T  D  E  Y  O  L  P  M  E  A  I  Z  T
B  O  R  I  S  I  S  A  L  I  A  R  X  V  N  P  P  C  H
W  B  F  D  L  Z  M  L  K  F  N  J  E  U  P  S  O  T  K
F  X  K  U  M  Y  K  T  X  Y  Y  Q  J  B  H  V  L  N  V
V  O  M  W  F  D  O  C  G  D  H  I  A  I  H  T  K  C  Q
W  O  P  D  P  A  Y  M  D  U  G  U  W  L  I  B  E  U  I
```

Download Festival 2022

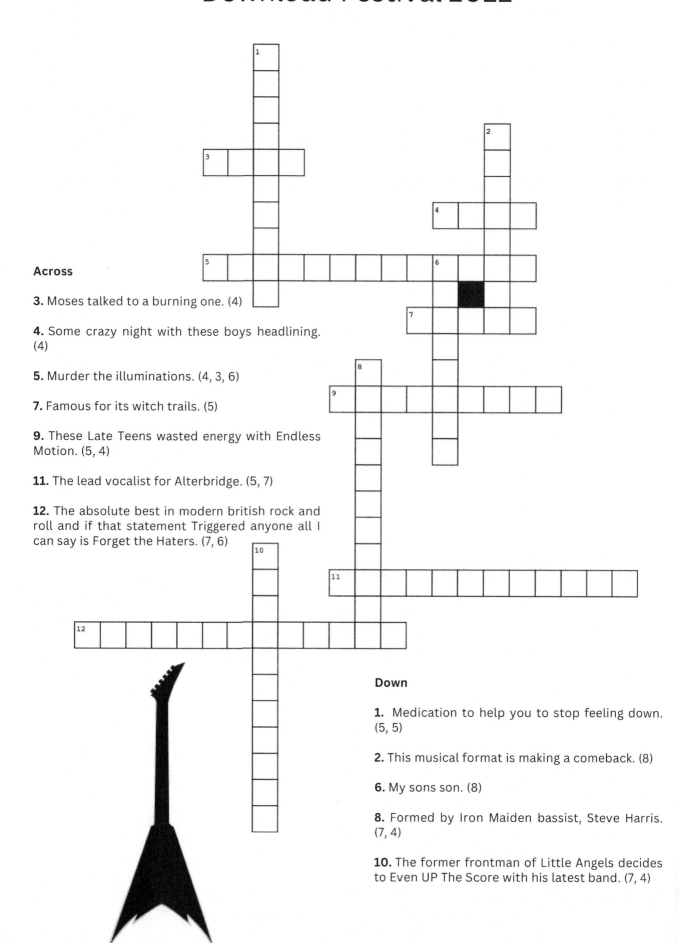

Across

3. Moses talked to a burning one. (4)

4. Some crazy night with these boys headlining. (4)

5. Murder the illuminations. (4, 3, 6)

7. Famous for its witch trails. (5)

9. These Late Teens wasted energy with Endless Motion. (5, 4)

11. The lead vocalist for Alterbridge. (5, 7)

12. The absolute best in modern british rock and roll and if that statement Triggered anyone all I can say is Forget the Haters. (7, 6)

Down

1. Medication to help you to stop feeling down. (5, 5)

2. This musical format is making a comeback. (8)

6. My sons son. (8)

8. Formed by Iron Maiden bassist, Steve Harris. (7, 4)

10. The former frontman of Little Angels decides to Even UP The Score with his latest band. (7, 4)

Download Festival 2022

See if you can find the acts from Download 2022 in the word search below. It is tricky though, words can be in any direction in a straight line, front or backward.

```
R  T  M  L  K  E  U  K  W  D  H  K  E  N  M  X  O  H  J
O  M  F  I  G  T  X  V  L  Q  Q  I  O  S  A  L  E  M  T
P  I  S  O  L  T  H  V  S  P  F  S  Z  P  S  A  I  R  C
O  S  Z  X  S  E  H  P  T  N  D  F  R  N  S  R  V  V  J
W  V  A  V  D  S  S  D  Z  N  O  E  T  I  I  K  L  P  E
Q  O  K  G  W  S  X  K  A  G  S  S  N  U  V  N  I  K  S
D  S  Q  O  K  A  F  R  E  S  T  I  D  J  E  F  W  I  D
C  Q  J  Y  G  C  G  L  C  N  K  M  X  R  W  Y  L  R  P
S  K  E  C  I  F  L  L  D  Z  N  W  F  K  A  B  T  A  B
J  R  G  S  C  C  U  V  E  S  X  E  F  O  G  W  R  I  V
H  T  J  V  L  B  M  K  R  Y  U  E  D  B  O  G  Y  L  H
S  T  H  G  I  L  E  H  T  L  L  I  K  Y  N  A  J  A  Z
N  O  I  L  H  S  I  T  I  R  B  G  P  O  S  J  H  S  W
R  F  K  Y  C  S  E  P  X  A  U  S  E  V  R  J  F  I  G
Q  F  N  E  K  L  H  Z  S  L  Y  G  S  R  O  L  X  S  Q
G  L  O  E  H  X  I  M  G  E  O  Z  M  N  C  G  K  I  E
J  Q  S  W  B  U  N  M  P  R  U  V  Z  Q  K  P  Q  R  O
M  D  G  X  M  R  E  Y  D  W  O  L  Y  N  M  S  S  O  E
S  V  W  W  E  O  U  Q  J  P  A  F  B  O  P  I  Z  B  G
```

Download Festival 2023

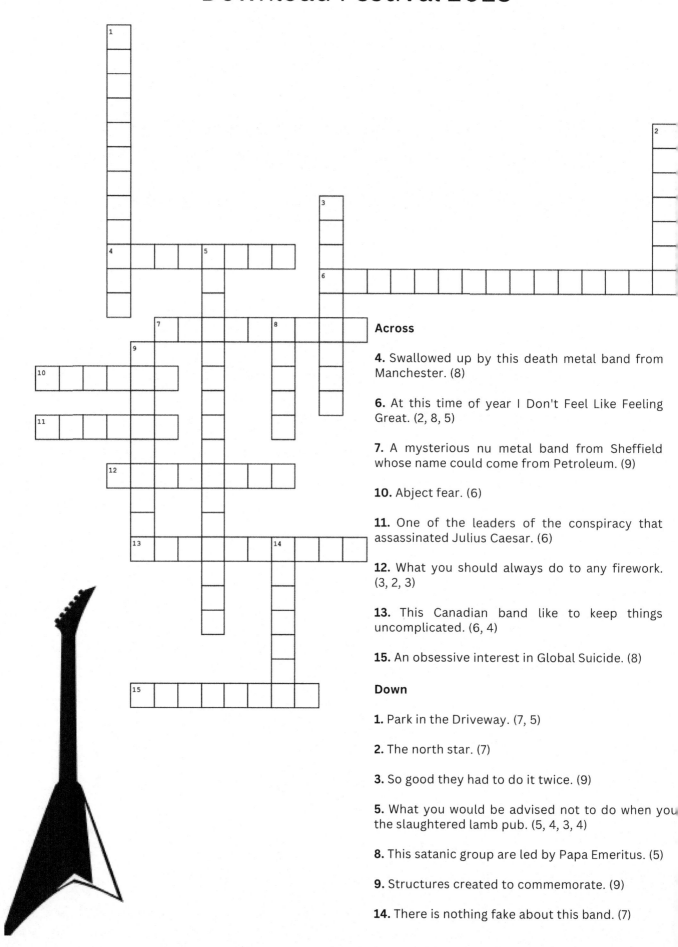

Across

4. Swallowed up by this death metal band from Manchester. (8)

6. At this time of year I Don't Feel Like Feeling Great. (2, 8, 5)

7. A mysterious nu metal band from Sheffield whose name could come from Petroleum. (9)

10. Abject fear. (6)

11. One of the leaders of the conspiracy that assassinated Julius Caesar. (6)

12. What you should always do to any firework. (3, 2, 3)

13. This Canadian band like to keep things uncomplicated. (6, 4)

15. An obsessive interest in Global Suicide. (8)

Down

1. Park in the Driveway. (7, 5)

2. The north star. (7)

3. So good they had to do it twice. (9)

5. What you would be advised not to do when you the slaughtered lamb pub. (5, 4, 3, 4)

8. This satanic group are led by Papa Emeritus. (5)

9. Structures created to commemorate. (9)

14. There is nothing fake about this band. (7)

Download Festival 2023

See if you can find the acts from Download 2023 in the word search below. It is tricky though, words can be in any direction in a straight line, front or backward.

```
D C Y M L G C J Y B X N H N P P R L L
S E Z N W C F F V A B A S P R X Q E X
N C T O Z E F X I K A L T C S M D L E
H N E S B C N G Z Q Z P R W O J W V I
D L Z S E E C M U K Q E A I C N H T V
B G S H E G C K G O U L Y S U T U R B
H R X C M T N A F G N P F M C X T A O
M O I M Y C I I L J H M R C K F C C C
M O N U M E N T S P M I O O P U L I C
E G W V F K T O O T Y S M E R K F L E
C P A Q B V B L S F I G T B H R M L C
J B K R G G A O K W F X H J V T E A N
C B F M G R H V J S F J E G C G P T O
V V B T I G T Y F W U S P B Y W M E I
H A E S Y B Z W Z L G O A T I N J M T
P A R K W A Y D R I V E T G D F D W A
B L A C K G O L D C K A H F X R W G X
D O L S L L A F R E B M E C E D S A I
R A I L A S I S I R O B E T C Z X R F
```

2003.

Across.
2. Soil. 4. Reef. 8. Violent Delight. 11. Flint. 12. The Darkness. 14. NOFX.

Down.
1. Ministry. 3. Marilyn Manson. 5. Evanescence. 6. Disturbed. 7. Chimaira. 9. Sepultura. 10. Thrice.
13. Deftones.

2004.

Across.
5. Korn. 7. Hurricane Party. 9. The Distillers. 13. Metallica. 14. Instruction. 15. Opeth. 16. Amplifier.

Down.
1. Cradle of Filth. 2. The Stooges. 3. Pennywise. 4. Slayer. 6. Dirty Americans. 8. Slipknot. 10. The Hives.
11. Peaches. 12. Recover.

2005.

Across.
2. Underoath. 4. Meshuggah. 7. Anthrax. 8. Garbage. 10. Black Sabbath. 11. Billy Idol. 13. Alter
Bridge. 15. Dwarves. 16. Mastodon. 18. Megadeth.

Down.
1. Flogging Molly. 3. Motorhead. 5. Helmet. 6. Napalm Death. 9. Tokyo Dragons. 12. Feeder.
14. Unearth. 17. Trivium.

2006.

Across.
1. Killing Joke. 3. Manic. 9. Bleeding Through. 13. Fishbone. 14. Tool. 15. Blindside. 16. Skindred.

Down.
2. Guns N Roses. 4. Cathedral. 5. Clutch. 6. The Audition. 7. From First to Last. 8. The Prodigy.
10. Darkest hour. 11. Alice in Chains. 12. Enter Shirkari.

2007.

Across.
4.Gallows. 6. Papa Roach. 9. Motley Crue. 11. Within Temptation. 14. Devildriver. 15. Velvet
Revolver.

Down.
1. Bowling for Soup. 2. Killswitch Engage. 3. Iron Maiden. 5. Wolfmother. 7. The Answer.
8. Architects. 10. Stone Sour. 12. Hayseed Dixie. 13. Dream Theatre.

2008.

Across.
3. Incubus. 4. Municipal Waste. 6. Kiss. 7. Testament. 9. Motorhead. 10. Pendulum. 12. Saxon.
13. Lost Prophets. 14. Offspring.

Down.
1. Kid Rock. 2. Judas Priest. 5. Jimmy Eat World. 8. Ash. 11. Exit Ten. 15. Finger Eleven.

2009.

Across.
4. Journey. 5. Thunder. 7. Limp Bizkit. 10. Def Leppard. 11. You Me At Six. 13. Blackhole.

Down.
1. Faith No More. 2. Anvil. 3. Chris Cornell. 6. Down. 8. ZZ Top. 9. Whitesnake. 12. Tesla.

2010.

Across.
2. Skin. 4. Aerosmith. 7. Zebrahead. 8. Halestorm. 9. Whitechapel. 10. Porcupine Tree. 11. ACDC. 12. Cinderella.

Down.
1. Stone Temple Pilots. 2. Steel Panther. 3. FM. 5. Them Crooked Vultures. 6. Volbeat.

2011.

Across.
4. Rob Zombie. 7. The Cult. 9. Ghost. 12. Deaf Havana. 13. Skunk Anansie. 15. Twisted Sister.

Down.
1. Alice Cooper. 2. Thin Lizzy. 3. System of a Down. 5. Mr Big. 6. Biohazard. 8. Plain White Ts. 10. Trash Talk. 11. Cheap Trick. 14. Frank Turner.

2012.

Across.
3. Metallica. 8. The Quireboys. 10. Biffy Clyro. 11. Tenacious D. 12. Rise Against. 15. Soundgarden.

Down.
1. Ugly Kid Joe. 2. Black Sabbath. 4. Billy Talent. 5. Shinedown. 6. Rival Sons. 7. Terrorvision. 9. Gun. 13. Fear Factory. 14. Axewound.

2013.

Across.
3. Bury Tomorrow. 6. Masters of Reality. 8. UFO. 10. Airbourne. 13. A Day to Remember.

Down.
1. Graveyard. 2. Cancer Bats. 4. Rammstein. 5. Katatonia. 7. Down. 9. Empress. 11. Uriah Heep. 12. Europe.

2014.

Across.
2. Nothing More. 3. Danger Danger. 8. Drenge. 10. Skillet. 11. Joe Bonamassa. 12. Fozzy. 13. Avatar.

Down.
1. Quicksand. 4. Richie Sambora. 5. Behemoth. 6. Winger. 7. Royal Blood. 9. Status Quo.

2015.

Across.
2. Ghost Town. 5. Yellowcard. 6. Muse. 7. Creeper. 8. Evil Scarecrow. 9. New Years day. 11. Crobot. 12. Decade. 13. Dub War.

Down.
1. Slash. 3. The Darkness. 4. Pop Evil. 10. All That Remains.

2016.

Across.
6. Inglorious. 8. Janes Addiction. 9. Tesseract. 11. Iron Maiden. 12. Heck

Down.
1. Monster Truck. 2. Electric Wizard. 3. Attila. 4. Glassjaw. 5. Milk Teeth. 7. Grand Magnus. 10. Kiss.

2017.

Across.
2. Of Mice and Men. 3. Sabaton. 5. Moses. 7. Red Fang. 8. Baroness. 11. Hacktivist. 12. Basement.

Down.
1. Perturbator. 4. The Contortionist. 6. Drones. 9. Exodus. 10. Slayer.

2018.

Across.
3. The Pink Slips. 4. Loathe. 7. Gold Key. 10. Mayday Parade. 11. Stick to Your Guns. 13. Ozzy Osbourne.

Down.
1. Puppy. 2. Jonathon Davis. 5. The Struts. 6. Higher Power. 8. The Bronx. 9. Neck Deep. 12. Guns N Roses.

2019.

Across.
3. Blurred Vision. 6. Smashing Pumpkins. 8. Amon Amarth. 9. Carcass. 10. Lovebites. 11. Coldrain.

Down.
1. Goodbye June. 2. Those Damn Crows. 4. Last in Line. 5. Skid Row. 7. Elvana. 9. Cloud.

2021.

Across.
2. Tigercub. 4. Hot Milk. 5. Jamie Lenman. 7. Malevolence. 9. The Wildhearts.

Down.
1. Massive Wagons. 3. Stone Broken. 6. Employed to Serve. 8. Trash Boat.

2022.

Across.
3. Bush. 4. Kiss. 5. Kill the Lights. 7. Salem. 9. Press Club. 11. Miles Kennedy. 12. Massive Wagons.

Down.
1. Blues Pills. 2. Cassette. 6. Grandson. 8. British Lion. 10. Wayward Sons.

2023.

Across.
4. Ingested. 6. As December Falls. 7. Blackgold. 10. Terror. 11. Brutus. 12. Set it Off. 13. Simple Plan. 15. Fixation.

Down.
1. Parkway Drive. 2. Polaris. 3. Metallica. 5. Stray from the Path. 8. Ghost. 9. Monuments. 14. Placebo.

Printed in Great Britain
by Amazon

35221081R00026